OSTRICHES

Rourke Enterprises, Inc.
Vero Beach, Florida 32964

PHOTO CREDITS
© Stephen J. Krasemann/DRK Photo: Cover;
© James P. Rowan: Pages 4, 7;
© Lynn M. Stone: all other photos

ACKNOWLEDGMENTS

The author wishes to thank the following for
photographic assistance in the preparation of this
book: Peter Arnold and The Ostrich Study Center,
Punta Gorda, Fla; The San Diego Ostrich Ranch;
The San Diego Wild Animal Park

Library of Congress Cataloging-in-Publication Data

Stone, Lynn M.
  Ostriches / by Lynn M. Stone

    p. cm. — (Bird discovery library)
    Includes index.
    Summary: Describes the appearance, habits, nesting, feedir
infancy, and importance to humans of the world's largest bird.
    ISBN 0-86592-323-X
    1. Ostriches—Juvenile literature. [1. Ostriches.] I. Title.
II. Series: Stone, Lynn M. Bird discovery library.
  QL696.S9S76 1989   598   88-30195
  598'.51 - dc19   st   CIP
                             Cil   AC

TABLE OF CONTENTS

OSTRICHES

The ostrich *(Struthio camelus)* is one of the world's most unusual birds. It is the largest bird on earth and the only one with just two toes on each foot.

They are taller and heavier than pro basketball players. Ostriches stand up to eight feet tall. Big male ostriches weigh over 300 pounds.

Ostriches have short, floppy wings and they can not fly. They depend on their long, strong legs to escape from enemies. An ostrich can run nearly 40 miles per hour.

The ostrich does not have any close relatives. Three other tall, **flightless** birds, however, look much like the ostrich. They are the emu, the rhea, and the cassowary.

Female (left) and Male
Ostriches

WHERE THEY LIVE

Wild ostriches live mainly in southern and eastern Africa. They like dry, open places where they can run easily and see for great distances. Ostriches do not hear very well, and they have a poor sense of smell. They do have excellent eyesight. The ostrich makes a good lookout for many of the other animals on the African **savannas,** or grassland.

Although it is not a cousin of the ostrich, the rhea is sometimes called "the ostrich of South America." The other two ostrich-like birds, the cassowary and emu, live in Australia.

Male Ostrich

HOW THEY LOOK

A male ostrich is a very impressive bird. He is so tall that the average person would need a stepladder to look him in the eye.

His neck is nearly four feet long. His legs are long and bare. His body is covered with black feathers trimmed by large, fluffy white feathers called **plumes.**

The female ostrich looks much like her mate, but she is smaller and her **plumage,** the covering of feathers, is gray-brown. Both male and female ostriches have big, dark eyes and long eyelashes.

THE OSTRICH'S EGGS

An ostrich egg is a marvel. It usually weighs almost three pounds and may be eight inches long. One ostrich egg can make the same size omelet as two dozen chicken eggs!

Ostrich eggs are cream-colored. Their thick shells have bumps like grapefruit skin.

For thousands of years, ostrich eggs have been used as ornaments and even drinking cups.

Egyptian vultures break into the ostrich eggs by throwing stones at them. Baby ostriches have a different problem: they have to break out of the egg! A baby ostrich uses its beak and toenails to hatch from the egg.

Ostrich Egg

Rhea (*Rhea americana*)
of South America

Emu
(Dromiceus novaehollandiae)
of Australia

THE OSTRICH'S DAY

Ostriches are active during daylight hours. They spend much of their time grazing with zebras, giraffes, wildebeestes, and other animals.

During the nesting season, the male and female ostriches take turns **incubating,** keeping the eggs warm.

People once thought ostriches buried their heads in the sand. That is not true, but nesting or napping ostriches may flatten their heads and necks on the ground. That makes them hard to see. From a distance, the ostrich appears to have lost—or buried—its head.

Ostrich Chick Napping

OSTRICH NESTS

Ostrich nests are shallow holes in the ground. Several hens lay in the same nest. Each ostrich hen lays six to eight eggs. The nest contains an average of 40 eggs. Only one pair of ostriches incubates the eggs, and a sitting ostrich can cover only about 20 eggs. The rest are pushed out of the nest.

The male ostrich incubates at night. The female incubates during the day, probably because her dull feathers help **camouflage,** or hide, her. The male's black plumage does not camouflage him well in daylight.

Ostrich Nest

BABY OSTRICHES

Six weeks after being laid, ostrich eggs hatch. The chicks are led quickly away from the nest by both parents.

Ostrich chicks are a foot tall at birth. They feed largely on plants and insects. Baby ostriches grow nearly a foot each month until they are six months old.

Gray feathers help camouflage baby ostriches. Even so, nine of every 10 ostrich chicks are killed by **predators,** animals that hunt other animals. Ostriches can live to be over 50 years old, but few reach even the age of one!

PREDATORS AND PREY

Baby ostriches are **prey,** or food, for many predators—jackals, lions, leopards, and other meat-eating animals. Adult ostriches are sometimes killed by predators, too. Usually, however, ostriches are too alert and too fast to be caught.

Adult ostriches are very strong. When they have babies to protect, they are very dangerous animals. Angry ostriches have killed young lions by kicking them to death.

Ostriches themselves eat fruits, seeds, grass, insects, lizards, snakes, and small furry animals. Captive ostriches have gobbled up coins, watches, and even nails.

Ostriches and African
Crowned Cranes

OSTRICHES AND PEOPLE

Ostriches have been important to people for centuries. Ostriches were trained thousands of years ago in Arabia, Egypt, and India. They hauled racing carts and even carried people on their backs. People ate ostrich meat, and their skin was used for leather. Their eggs were used for food, decorations, and cups.

In the late 1800's, women wore ostrich plumes on their hats. The best ostrich feathers cost up to $500 a pound. People began to raise ostriches on farms.

Today ostrich plumes and ostrich meat are not in fashion. Ostrich eggs and skin—leather—remain valuable. Ostriches are still raised on a few farms in South Africa, Australia, and the United States.

GLOSSARY

Camouflage (KAM oh flage)—to hide by matching an animal's color to its surroundings

Flightless (FLITE less)—a bird without the ability to fly, such as ostriches and penguins

Incubate (INK you bate) incubating—to keep eggs warm until they hatch

Plumes (PLOOMZ)—long, soft, fancy feathers

Plumage (PLOO maj)—the covering of feathers on a bird

Predator (PRED a tor)—an animal that kills another animal for food

Prey (PRAY)—an animal that is hunted for food by another animal

Savannas (sa VAN nuhz)—broad, grassy areas with few trees; a grassland

INDEX